The Science of Gravity

John Stringer

WAYLAND

Science World

Other titles in the series:

The Science of a
Light Bulb

The Science of
Noise

The Science of a
Spring

Picture acknowledgements
Wayland Publishers would like to thank the following for allowing their pictures to be reproduced in this book:
Eye Ubiquitous 12, /Adina Tovy Amsel 16 (bottom), /A.J.G. Bell 14, /NASA *cover* (main), 10, 18; Genesis 4;
Getty Images/Ken Fisher *title page*, 24, /Dan Ham *cover* (inset top), /Chris Noble 15, /Mark Wagner 7, /Tim
Young 8; Angela Hampton *cover* (inset middle), 6 (top); Science Photo Library/John Bavesi 16 (top), /NASA 17,
19 (both), /Novosti 21, /David Nunuk 22, /Bill Sanderson 6 (bottom), /Kaj R. Svensson *contents page*, 20, /Jerry
Wachter 23; Wayland Picture Library 5 (all), 9, 11.

The illustrations on pages 28 and 29 are by Peter Bull.
The illustrations on pages 13, 25, 26 and 27 are by Rudi Vizi.

Editor: Carron Brown
Consultant: Anne Goldsworthy
Series design: Lisa Nutt
Designer: Mark Whitchurch
Production controller: Carol Stevens

First published in 1999 by Wayland Publishers Ltd,
61 Western Road, Hove, East Sussex BN3 1JD

This edition published in 2000 by Wayland
Publishers Ltd

British Library in Cataloguing Data
Stringer, John
  The Science of Gravity. – (Science World)
  1. Gravity – Juvenile literature
  I. Title
  531.1'4

ISBN 0 7502 2406 1

Find Wayland on the Internet at http://www.wayland.co.uk

Contents

What is gravity?   4

How does gravity affect you?   10

Gravity above the surface   24

Glossary   30

Further information/Topic web   31

Index   32

What is gravity?

Gravity is an invisible force that pulls together any two objects. It pulls us down towards our planet, Earth, and holds us there. We can't see it, but we can see its effects.

Why don't we always feel the pulling force of gravity? Usually the force is too weak to feel, but it gets stronger the more massive something is. So what's massive and very close to you? It's the planet we live on, the Earth. That's why you can feel the pull between you and the Earth.

▼ Only the Earth is massive enough to have a force of gravity we can feel.

The strength of gravity's pull

How strong is the pull of gravity in these pictures? Is it weak? Or is it strong? (Clue: look at the mass of the objects.)

◀ There is a strong pull of gravity between the bulls and the ground.

There is a strong pull of ▶ gravity between the castle and the ground.

▼ The pull of gravity between these two people is weak.

▼ The pull of gravity between the flower and the butterfly is weak.

Falling

Have you ever wondered why something falls down when you drop it, and not sideways or up? Objects fall down because of the force of gravity pulling them towards the centre of the Earth.

When you throw a ball into the air, ▶ the force of gravity pulls it down towards the ground.

Sir Isaac Newton and gravity

Sir Isaac Newton was a famous scientist who lived 300 years ago. There is a story that says that he saw an apple fall from a tree and it started him thinking. 'Why does everything fall downwards? It's as if there is a force pulling everything towards the centre of the Earth.' The pulling force he thought about is called gravity. He thought that everything that had mass was attracted to everything else.

Any two objects have a force of gravity between them. You and everything around you is affected by gravity. Objects that are massive have more gravity between them than less massive objects. The Earth is so massive that it pulls everything downwards. It's just as well. Without gravity, you would float off into space.

Some ferries are huge. ▶ They are nowhere near as massive as the Earth but, when two ferries are docked next to each other, they are pulled together by the force of gravity between them.

Moving objects without touching them

There are other invisible forces like gravity. Magnetism is an invisible force. Magnets can pull objects without touching them. Magnets pull objects made of iron and steel, and some other metals.

Sometimes magnets can pull other magnets towards them. Sometimes they can push other magnets away from them.

▼ The force of magnetism has pulled these metal paper clips on to a magnet.

Magnets can work through other materials. You can move paper clips around with a magnet under the table. A strong magnet will even pull through your hand and will work through air and water.

How does gravity compare with magnetism?

Force	Can it pull objects together?	Can it push objects apart?	Is it invisible?	Will it work with any two objects?
Gravity	Yes	No	Yes	Yes
Magnetism	Yes	Yes	Yes	No

In some ways, gravity is like magnetism. It is also invisible and it works without touching. Even if you are flying in an aeroplane or swimming in the sea, gravity is still pulling you down.

◄ You can create a chain of paper clips by holding a magnet above a pile of paper clips. You will notice that the paper clips move towards the magnet, drawn by its attraction. The magnetism travels through each paper clip attached to the magnet. Soon you will have a chain.

How does gravity affect you?

You need muscles and bones to keep your body shape against the pull of gravity. Without gravity, you would have no weight and you would float off into space.

▼ When in space, astronauts can float around because there is almost no gravity to give them weight.

Weight and mass

The pull of the Earth is strong for two reasons. The Earth is very, very massive, it weighs about six billion trillion tonnes, and you are standing on it. The Earth's gravity is pulling down on you all the time. We call that pull your weight.

Collapsing men from Mars!

The science fiction writer H.G. Wells wrote a famous book about an invasion of the Earth by Martians, called *The War Of The Worlds*. In it, the Martians had to build themselves machines for walking around. Because gravity is much less forceful on Mars, their bodies weren't strong enough for Earth's gravity!

When you hold a ball, you can feel the ▶ weight of it in your hand. This is because gravity is pulling the ball into your hand giving it weight.

Losing weight but not mass!

You have weight because of the pull between you and the Earth. The mass is what you are made from. Your mass stays the same, wherever you are, but if you go to the moon or a planet, your weight can change.

▼ This astronaut has almost no weight while he is floating around in space, but his body, his mass, remains the same.

Does your weight change on the Moon?

The Earth has about six times more mass than our Moon. When astronauts went there, their mass stayed the same; but the pull between them and the Moon was about six times less than the pull between them and the Earth. Their weight on the moon was one-sixth of their weight on Earth, so they could leap around like grasshoppers!

If you went to another planet, the pull of gravity would change. If the planet was more massive than the Earth, the pull would be stronger. If the planet were less massive than the Earth, the pull would be weaker.

Gravity is like a bungee jump in ▶ reverse. When you leave the Earth, gravity pulls you back. (Though unlike a bungee jump, it doesn't pull harder the further you go.)

On a tiny planet, the pull of ▶ gravity is so small that you could easily jump very high.

On a huge planet the ▶ pull of gravity would drag you down. You would feel heavy and find it hard to jump.

Lighter up a mountain

You have weight because of the pull between your mass and the Earth's mass. Your mass stays the same, wherever you are. However, your weight can change if you get further away from the centre of the Earth.

▼ The nearer you are to the centre of the Earth, the more you weigh. At the bottom of a valley, you weigh a little more than you weigh at the top!

▼ The further you are from the centre of the Earth, the less you will weigh. Climb to the top of a mountain and you lose weight – but not mass. The bathroom scales will still give you the same reading when you come down.

Weightlessness

Have you ever been over a hump-backed bridge in a car or been on a fast, bumpy fairground ride? For a moment, you may have felt as if you had no weight. This is how you would feel if there was no gravity on our planet to give you weight and keep you on the ground.

▼ You feel weightless on a big wheel when you're spun round the top, travelling back down to the bottom.

In your backbone, ▶ there are large bones called vertebrae that are held apart by squishy, soft discs. On Earth, gravity squashes the soft discs. When you are weightless, the discs are not squashed as much. You actually become almost two centimetres or so taller!

If you go far enough into space, you can be so far from any planets or stars that their gravity hardly affects you. You become almost weightless. Your body will still have the same mass but, because there is almost no pull of gravity, you will float around with no up or down.

▼ In a space shuttle an astronaut can float upside-down, while another astronaut is upright!

Living in space

Astronauts who have been weightless for some time notice some strange changes to their bodies. The blood inside you is pumped by your heart so it can flow to each part of your body. When weightless, astronauts' blood is still being pumped 'up' to their head but there is no gravity to pull the blood back down, so their faces swell. Also, they aren't using their legs to hold their bodies up, so their muscles and bones get weaker. After some time in the new conditions, their bodies adjust.

▲ The heart of an astronaut beats ten times a minute slower after being weightless for a while.

This astronaut is chasing a weightless ▶ sandwich around his living area.

While in space, every object floats that isn't anchored down. Astronauts have to be careful when they move around their living area as objects are still the same mass and large objects could hurt if they bang into them.

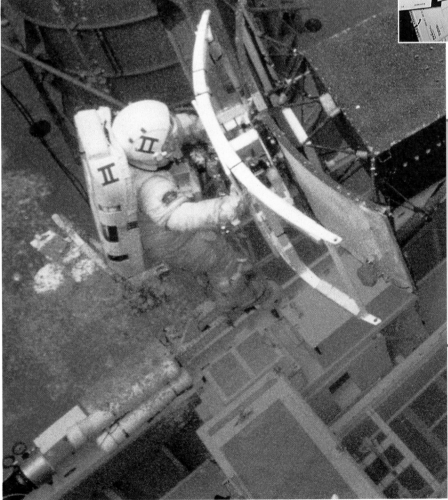

◀ Astronauts train underwater to create weightlessness effects similar to space. This means that they can learn how to move in weightless conditions.

Other strong forces

Sometimes we feel strong forces, such as when we are on a fairground ride, or take a tight corner in a car. Your body keeps moving in one direction while the car or fairground ride moves suddenly in a different direction. This can make you feel dizzy or even sick.

▼ When you go on fairground rides that go upside-down and swing you from side to side at a fast speed, you feel strong forces acting on you.

Your ear is the organ that senses the pull of gravity. It has fluid-filled spaces called semi-circular canals. The fluid moves about as you move and bends tiny hairs that tell the brain what direction you're leaning towards and if you're upright. If you are weightless, or when you are affected by very strong forces, you may feel sick when the brain can't make sense of the messages.

How do you get used to strong forces?

Pilots and astronauts are trained to become used to strong forces. They may ride on the end of a huge roundabout that spins them faster and faster. They feel a force several times the force of their own weight.

Centre of gravity

Every object has its mass and weight concentrated on one point. This imaginary point is called the centre of gravity. Exactly where the centre of gravity is depends on the object's shape. A tall object with most of its mass at the top has a high centre of gravity. A short object with its mass concentrated at the base has a low centre of gravity.

◀ Objects with a high centre of gravity are more likely to topple over than objects with a low centre of gravity. Tall vehicles, such as lorries, have all their heavy bits, the engine and axles, as low as possible to create a low centre of gravity. This lorry would have to lean a long way to fall over as its centre of gravity is close to the ground.

If you could drill a hole right through the centre of the Earth and come out the other side, you would drill right through the Earth's centre of gravity.

▲ This gymnast is constantly changing her position as she moves. She balances more easily when her centre of gravity is low down – close to the bar. When she stands on her feet, her centre of gravity is high up and she finds balancing harder. When she does a handstand, her centre of gravity is higher up and it is even harder for her to keep balance.

If you dropped a ball down the hole, it would travel back and forth through the hole until it came to rest in the very middle – the Earth's centre of gravity.

Gravity above the Earth's surface

Gravity still pulls on objects when they aren't on the Earth's surface. Everything above you, for example, aircraft, birds and even the moon, is affected by gravity's pull. In fact, everything in the air above the Earth is falling. But they don't all fall to the ground with a bump because many objects use speed and air resistance to fly and land safely.

These people are jumping ▶ out of an aeroplane way above the ground. Each person has a parachute in a bag on his or her back. Pulling a string releases the parachute from the bag allowing them to fall down safely to the ground.

Friction of air moving across the parachute, inside and outside, helps slow down the fall.

Air slows you down in two ways. Firstly, the parachute fills with air and the air pushes up on the parachute. Secondly, the air slips over the surface of the parachute and the drag of it holds you back. This is called air resistance.

The trapped air escapes through a small central hole. This stops the parachute swinging and 'spilling' out the air, making the parachutist feel sick.

The parachutist is pulled towards the centre of the Earth by the force of gravity.

Staying up

Stand by for take-off. Stand by for the great tug of war. On the down team – gravity! On the up team, the lift from the aeroplane. But how will we give the aeroplane lift? Of course! Engines to full throttle. If enough air flows over the wings, fast enough, the aeroplane will go up.

▲ We're rushing forward. Air is streaming over the wings. Because of their special shape, they're giving us lift. Gravity is losing. The aeroplane is climbing.

How do gliders stay in the air?

Gliders can stay in the air without an engine for a long time. Gliders use their long wings to soar up on thermals – huge columns of rising air. Without the thermals, gravity would pull the glider down.

▲ Whoops! We're out of petrol. The aeroplane is slowing down. The air over the wings is slowing down, too. We haven't enough lift. Gravity is winning! Stand by for a crash landing!

Gravity's pull on the planets

The planets in our solar system are moving around the Sun, kept in orbit by gravity. Some of the planets have moons orbiting around them. Others have rings. All these are held in space by the forces of gravity.

▼ This picture shows the Sun and the planets in our solar system. You can see the thick rings around Saturn.

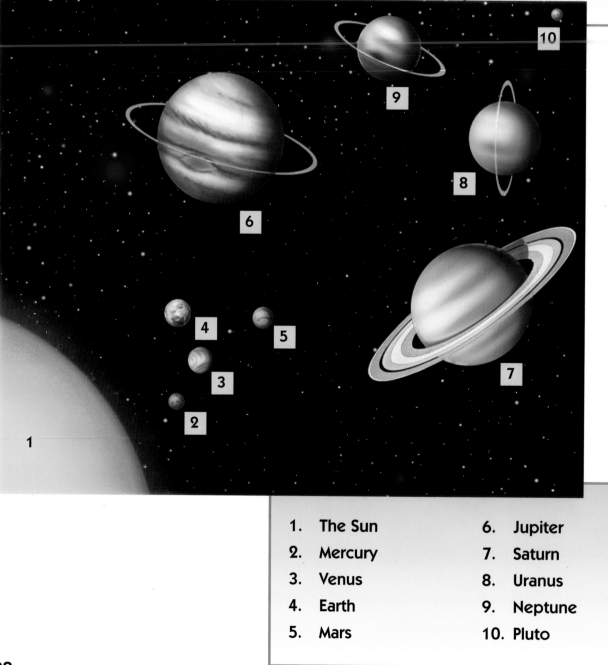

1.	The Sun	6.	Jupiter
2.	Mercury	7.	Saturn
3.	Venus	8.	Uranus
4.	Earth	9.	Neptune
5.	Mars	10.	Pluto

▲ Pluto (left) and Charon (right) in orbit. They both orbit the same point. It's as if the two planets are holding hands and swinging round in a circle.

The Earth's Moon orbits the Earth's centre of gravity. The planet Pluto has such a massive moon, Charon, that Pluto and Charon are nearly the same mass. As they both equal the same mass, they both orbit a point in space between them, like a pair of dancers holding hands.

What are black holes?

A black hole is caused by a very dense massive object that has a huge gravitational pull. This acts like a space funnel. Anything pulled into the space funnel can never escape.

Glossary

Air resistance The slowing down force of air on moving objects.

Astronauts Members of a crew on a spacecraft.

Centre of gravity The point in an object where its weight is evenly balanced.

Force A push or a pull between objects.

Gravity The force of attraction between two objects. The greater their mass, and the closer they are, the greater the force of gravity between them.

Gravitational Having something to do with gravity.

Magnetic field The area around a magnet where the magnetic effect can be detected.

Magnetism The invisible force of a magnet. It is strongest at the ends, or poles, of a magnet.

Mass The amount of matter in something. The mass of something never changes; its weight will change with a different force of gravity.

Muscles Strong body tissue that can get shorter and longer, and so allows us to move parts of the body.

Resistance Something that tends to stop movement. so air resistance is the slowing-down force of air.

Weight The force exerted on an object by the Earth. An object's weight depends upon its mass.

Weightlessness When you are in space, far from the gravitational pull of the stars and planets, you are almost weightless.

Further Information

Books to read

Fatal Forces (*Horrible Science* series)
by Nick Arnold (Scholastic, 1997)

Forces (*Essential Science Cards*) by John Stringer
and Michael Ward (Channel 4 Learning 1999)

Forces (*Star Science* series) – books for infants,
lower and upper juniors – by Rosemary Feasey,
Anne Goldsworthy, Roy Phipps and
John Stringer (Ginn, 1998)

Forces and Movement (*Straightforward Science*
series) by Peter Riley (Watts, 1998)

I Ddn't Know You Could Jump Higher on the Moon
by Kate Perry (Watts, 1997)

Machines (*Connections* series)
by Caroline Grimshaw (Two-Can, 1997)

Space Travel by Jan Oxlade (Watts, 1994)

Websites to visit

www.nmsi.ac.uk/welcome.html
This is the home page of the Science Museum.

www.askeric.org/Projects/Newton
This site contains many interesting science
lessons.

Places to visit

The Science Museum, Exhibition Road, South
Kensington, London (Tel: 0171 938 8000).

Woolsthorpe Manor, Grantham, Lincolnshire,
UK (Tel: 01476 860338) is Isaac Newton's home,
where he made many of his discoveries.

Gravity TOPIC WEB

MUSIC
• Compose a piece of music that describes falling or floating down to the ground.

GEOGRAPHY
• Look at your local area and think about the places where you would weigh most (i.e. on top of a hill) and least (i.e. valley).

HISTORY
• Find out about the story of Sir Isaac Newton and his discoveries.

ART AND CRAFT
• Make different-shaped objects out of plasticine experimenting with different centres of gravity.

DESIGN AND TECHNOLOGY
• Look at different objects and how they are designed to stop them from falling over.
• Investigate how objects and astronauts are 'held down' whilst in space.
• Look at objects that fly and float in the air and explain why their design helps them.

SCIENCE
• Explore pushes and pulls – look at how different forces work.
• Investigate different centres of gravity.
• Investigate air resistance, drag.

ENGLISH
• Write an article about the importance of gravity, gravity on different planets and about being weightless.

MATHS
• Look at measurement: e.g. newtons, weight, mass.

Index

Numbers in **bold** refer to pictures as well as text.

aeroplanes 9, 24, **26–7**

air 24, 25, 26–7

air resistance 24–5, 30

astronauts **10**, **12**, **13**, **17–19**,
    21, 30

backbones **16**

black holes 29

body shapes 10, 16, 18

centre of gravity 22–3, 30

ears 21

Earth **4**, 11, 23, **28**, 29

fairground rides **16**, **20**

falling **6**

forces, strong 20–21

gliders 27

gymnasts **23**

magnetism **8–9**, 30

mass 6, 7, 12, 13, 14, 17, 30

moons 12, 13, 28, 29

Newton, Sir Isaac **6**

parachutes 24, **25**

pilots 21

planets 12, **13**, **28–9**

sick, feeling 20, 21, 25

space **10**, **11**, **17–19**, 21, **28–9**

vehicles **22**

weight 10–15, 30

weightlessness **10**, 16–19, 30

Wells, H. G. 11